The Integrity Driven Le

How to Use the Integrity Driven Le

This Journal is broken into three core sections: Once-A-Quarter, Bi-Weekly, and Daily (M-F). Each journal will last you three months of your year.

Once-a-Quarter: This section is designed to help you continue to identify and refine your purpose, your 10-year vision, and your goals for the year. By revisiting it every quarter, at the start of each new journal, you will ensure that you are staying on track and giving yourself the opportunity to course correct as needed. Reach out to your coach if you are having trouble identifying your purpose, 10-year vision or goals for the year.

Bi-Weekly: This section is designed to keep you in lockstep with your coaching program. You will recap your action items so they stay in front of you, hone in on your inspirational focus (a person, a mantra, a set of ideals, scripture, a quote, etc.), identify your next steps for growth, and review your team strengths and opportunities. This is formulated to help you look for wins and seek conscious areas for improvement.

Daily (M-F): The daily section is all about consistency and focus. Each section will help you drive incremental progress toward your goals. The bullet list helps you assess your daily habits. Practicing gratitude and recognizing wins enables you to maintain proper perspective while developing resiliency. Daily meetings & priorities and weekly wins allows you create a positive feedback loop in your week.

We are excited to be on this journey with you!

The Integrity Driven Leader

The 5 Elements of Creating a Strong Purpose

Inspirational: It makes you feel unstoppable; it's your reason to jump out of bed in the morning.
Impactful: It challenges you to make a difference to others but is not dependent on specific people.
Universal: It spans across all areas of your life; it is not dependent on a set of circumstances.
Aspirational: It describes the person you want to be and the impact you want to have; it's not who you are yet.
Controllable: At the end of the day you can ask, "Did I live according to my purpose?" You have to live it out.

Questions to Uncover Your 10-Year Vision

- Where do you see yourself in 10 years?
- How much income do you want to bring in?
- What does your lifestyle look like?
- What does your overall financial picture look like?
- What sort of hobbies do you want to engage in?
- Where do you want to have traveled?
- What relationships are important to you?
- What do you see yourself doing for work?
- What does your ideal day look like?
- What do people say about you?
- How are you involved in your community?
- In what ways are you a steward of your gifts and resources?
- What have you accomplished by then?
- What do you still want to accomplish?
- Where do you have real estate or investments?
- What does your family dynamic look like?
- What experiences have you had?
- What are you proud of?
- What brings you joy?
- What does your health look like?
- What does your spiritual practice look like?
- What are you known for?
- How have you impacted those around you?
- What drives you to excellence?
- What values do you espouse?

Questions to Uncover Your One-Year Goals

- Where do you see yourself in 1 year?
- What exercise habits do you want?
- What stretching/mobility/flexibility habits do you want?
- What reading habits do you want?
- What prayer/meditation habits do you want?
- What water/hydration habits do you want?
- What dietary habits do you want?
- What TV/Social media habits do you want?
- What moderation/elimination of alcohol/vices do you want?
- What ways do you want to give recognition and to whom?
- What relationships do you want to invest in?
- What ways do you want to become more emotionally intelligent?
- With whom do you need to improve candid conversations?
- In what areas do you want to become more self-accountable?
- In what areas do you want to act with the highest integrity?
- In what areas do you want to demonstrate perseverance?
- What financial choices align with your goals?
- What do you want your generosity or charitable giving to look like?

The Integrity Driven Leader

My Purpose

My 10-Year Vision

My One-Year Goals

The Integrity Driven Leader

Coaching Action Items

Date Assigned:

Due Date:

Notes:

- ○
- ○
- ○
- ○
- ○

Inspiration

Areas of Personal Growth

- ○
- ○
- ○
- ○
- ○
- ○
- ○
- ○

Team Strengths this Period

- ○
- ○
- ○
- ○

Team Opportunities this Period

- ○
- ○
- ○
- ○

The Integrity Driven Leader

Today's Priorities

- ○
- ○
- ○
- ○
- ○
- ○
- ○
- ○
- ○
- ○

Gratitude

Meetings & Personal Conferences

- ○
- ○
- ○
- ○
- ○
- ○

Daily Practice

- ○ Exercise/Stretch
- ○ Read/Audio Book
- ○ Pray/Meditate
- ○ Give Recognition
- ○ Relationship Time
- ○ Emotional Intelligence
- ○ Candid Conversations
- ○ Self-Accountability
- ○ Integrity
- ○ Perseverence
- ○ Wise Financial Choices
- ○ Charity/Generosity
- ○ Water Intake
- ○ Eat Right
- ○ Limit TV/Social Media
- ○ Limit Alcohol/Vices
- ○ Healthy Sleep

Goals for the Weeks

Affirmations

Wins From Today

The Integrity Driven Leader

Today's Priorities

Gratitude

Meetings & Personal Conferences

Daily Practice

- Exercise/Stretch
- Read/Audio Book
- Pray/Meditate
- Give Recognition
- Relationship Time
- Emotional Intelligence
- Candid Conversations
- Self-Accountability
- Integrity
- Perseverence
- Wise Financial Choices
- Charity/Generosity
- Water Intake
- Eat Right
- Limit TV/Social Media
- Limit Alcohol/Vices
- Healthy Sleep

Goals for the Weeks

Affirmations

Wins From Today

The Integrity Driven Leader

Today's Priorities

- ○
- ○
- ○
- ○
- ○
- ○
- ○
- ○
- ○
- ○

Gratitude

Meetings & Personal Conferences

- ○
- ○
- ○
- ○
- ○
- ○

Daily Practice

- ○ Exercise/Stretch
- ○ Read/Audio Book
- ○ Pray/Meditate
- ○ Give Recognition
- ○ Relationship Time
- ○ Emotional Intelligence
- ○ Candid Conversations
- ○ Self-Accountability
- ○ Integrity
- ○ Perseverence
- ○ Wise Financial Choices
- ○ Charity/Generosity
- ○ Water Intake
- ○ Eat Right
- ○ Limit TV/Social Media
- ○ Limit Alcohol/Vices
- ○ Healthy Sleep

Goals for the Weeks

Affirmations

Wins From Today

The Integrity Driven Leader

Today's Priorities

- ○
- ○
- ○
- ○
- ○
- ○
- ○
- ○
- ○
- ○

Gratitude

Meetings & Personal Conferences

- ○
- ○
- ○
- ○
- ○
- ○

Daily Practice

- ○ Exercise/Stretch
- ○ Read/Audio Book
- ○ Pray/Meditate
- ○ Give Recognition
- ○ Relationship Time
- ○ Emotional Intelligence
- ○ Candid Conversations
- ○ Self-Accountability
- ○ Integrity
- ○ Perseverence
- ○ Wise Financial Choices
- ○ Charity/Generosity
- ○ Water Intake
- ○ Eat Right
- ○ Limit TV/Social Media
- ○ Limit Alcohol/Vices
- ○ Healthy Sleep

Goals for the Weeks

Affirmations

Wins From Today

The Integrity Driven Leader

Today's Priorities

- ○
- ○
- ○
- ○
- ○
- ○
- ○
- ○
- ○
- ○

Gratitude

Meetings & Personal Conferences

- ○
- ○
- ○
- ○
- ○
- ○

Daily Practice

- ○ Exercise/Stretch
- ○ Read/Audio Book
- ○ Pray/Meditate
- ○ Give Recognition
- ○ Relationship Time
- ○ Emotional Intelligence
- ○ Candid Conversations
- ○ Self-Accountability
- ○ Integrity
- ○ Perseverence
- ○ Wise Financial Choices
- ○ Charity/Generosity
- ○ Water Intake
- ○ Eat Right
- ○ Limit TV/Social Media
- ○ Limit Alcohol/Vices
- ○ Healthy Sleep

Goals for the Weeks

Affirmations

Wins From Today

The Integrity Driven Leader

Today's Priorities

- ○
- ○
- ○
- ○
- ○
- ○
- ○
- ○
- ○
- ○

Gratitude

Meetings & Personal Conferences

- ○
- ○
- ○
- ○
- ○
- ○

Daily Practice

- ○ Exercise/Stretch
- ○ Read/Audio Book
- ○ Pray/Meditate
- ○ Give Recognition
- ○ Relationship Time
- ○ Emotional Intelligence
- ○ Candid Conversations
- ○ Self-Accountability
- ○ Integrity
- ○ Perseverence
- ○ Wise Financial Choices
- ○ Charity/Generosity
- ○ Water Intake
- ○ Eat Right
- ○ Limit TV/Social Media
- ○ Limit Alcohol/Vices
- ○ Healthy Sleep

Goals for the Weeks

Affirmations

Wins From Today

The Integrity Driven Leader

Today's Priorities

- ○
- ○
- ○
- ○
- ○
- ○
- ○
- ○
- ○
- ○

Gratitude

Meetings & Personal Conferences

- ○
- ○
- ○
- ○
- ○
- ○

Daily Practice

- ○ Exercise/Stretch
- ○ Read/Audio Book
- ○ Pray/Meditate
- ○ Give Recognition
- ○ Relationship Time
- ○ Emotional Intelligence
- ○ Candid Conversations
- ○ Self-Accountability
- ○ Integrity
- ○ Perseverence
- ○ Wise Financial Choices
- ○ Charity/Generosity
- ○ Water Intake
- ○ Eat Right
- ○ Limit TV/Social Media
- ○ Limit Alcohol/Vices
- ○ Healthy Sleep

Goals for the Weeks

Affirmations

Wins From Today

The Integrity Driven Leader

Today's Priorities

Gratitude

Meetings & Personal Conferences

Daily Practice

- Exercise/Stretch
- Read/Audio Book
- Pray/Meditate
- Give Recognition
- Relationship Time
- Emotional Intelligence
- Candid Conversations
- Self-Accountability
- Integrity
- Perseverence
- Wise Financial Choices
- Charity/Generosity
- Water Intake
- Eat Right
- Limit TV/Social Media
- Limit Alcohol/Vices
- Healthy Sleep

Goals for the Weeks

Affirmations

Wins From Today

The Integrity Driven Leader

Today's Priorities

- ○
- ○
- ○
- ○
- ○
- ○
- ○
- ○
- ○
- ○

Gratitude

Meetings & Personal Conferences

- ○
- ○
- ○
- ○
- ○
- ○

Daily Practice

- ○ Exercise/Stretch
- ○ Read/Audio Book
- ○ Pray/Meditate
- ○ Give Recognition
- ○ Relationship Time
- ○ Emotional Intelligence
- ○ Candid Conversations
- ○ Self-Accountability
- ○ Integrity
- ○ Perseverence
- ○ Wise Financial Choices
- ○ Charity/Generosity
- ○ Water Intake
- ○ Eat Right
- ○ Limit TV/Social Media
- ○ Limit Alcohol/Vices
- ○ Healthy Sleep

Goals for the Weeks

Affirmations

Wins From Today

The Integrity Driven Leader

Today's Priorities

Gratitude

Meetings & Personal Conferences

Daily Practice

- Exercise/Stretch
- Read/Audio Book
- Pray/Meditate
- Give Recognition
- Relationship Time
- Emotional Intelligence
- Candid Conversations
- Self-Accountability
- Integrity
- Perseverence
- Wise Financial Choices
- Charity/Generosity
- Water Intake
- Eat Right
- Limit TV/Social Media
- Limit Alcohol/Vices
- Healthy Sleep

Goals for the Weeks

Affirmations

Wins From Today

The Integrity Driven Leader

Coaching Action Items

Date Assigned:

Due Date:

Notes:

- ○
- ○
- ○
- ○
- ○

Inspiration

Areas of Personal Growth

- ○
- ○
- ○
- ○
- ○
- ○
- ○
- ○

Team Strengths this Period

- ○
- ○
- ○
- ○

Team Opportunities this Period

- ○
- ○
- ○
- ○

The Integrity Driven Leader

Today's Priorities

- ○
- ○
- ○
- ○
- ○
- ○
- ○
- ○
- ○
- ○

Gratitude

Meetings & Personal Conferences

- ○
- ○
- ○
- ○
- ○
- ○

Daily Practice

- ○ Exercise/Stretch
- ○ Read/Audio Book
- ○ Pray/Meditate
- ○ Give Recognition
- ○ Relationship Time
- ○ Emotional Intelligence
- ○ Candid Conversations
- ○ Self-Accountability
- ○ Integrity
- ○ Perseverence
- ○ Wise Financial Choices
- ○ Charity/Generosity
- ○ Water Intake
- ○ Eat Right
- ○ Limit TV/Social Media
- ○ Limit Alcohol/Vices
- ○ Healthy Sleep

Goals for the Weeks

Affirmations

Wins From Today

The Integrity Driven Leader

Today's Priorities

Gratitude

Meetings & Personal Conferences

Daily Practice

- Exercise/Stretch
- Read/Audio Book
- Pray/Meditate
- Give Recognition
- Relationship Time
- Emotional Intelligence
- Candid Conversations
- Self-Accountability
- Integrity
- Perseverence
- Wise Financial Choices
- Charity/Generosity
- Water Intake
- Eat Right
- Limit TV/Social Media
- Limit Alcohol/Vices
- Healthy Sleep

Goals for the Weeks

Affirmations

Wins From Today

The Integrity Driven Leader

Today's Priorities

Gratitude

Meetings & Personal Conferences

Daily Practice

- Exercise/Stretch
- Read/Audio Book
- Pray/Meditate
- Give Recognition
- Relationship Time
- Emotional Intelligence
- Candid Conversations
- Self-Accountability
- Integrity
- Perseverence
- Wise Financial Choices
- Charity/Generosity
- Water Intake
- Eat Right
- Limit TV/Social Media
- Limit Alcohol/Vices
- Healthy Sleep

Goals for the Weeks

Affirmations

Wins From Today

The Integrity Driven Leader

Today's Priorities

- ○
- ○
- ○
- ○
- ○
- ○
- ○
- ○
- ○
- ○

Gratitude

Meetings & Personal Conferences

- ○
- ○
- ○
- ○
- ○
- ○

Daily Practice

- ○ Exercise/Stretch
- ○ Read/Audio Book
- ○ Pray/Meditate
- ○ Give Recognition
- ○ Relationship Time
- ○ Emotional Intelligence
- ○ Candid Conversations
- ○ Self-Accountability
- ○ Integrity
- ○ Perseverence
- ○ Wise Financial Choices
- ○ Charity/Generosity
- ○ Water Intake
- ○ Eat Right
- ○ Limit TV/Social Media
- ○ Limit Alcohol/Vices
- ○ Healthy Sleep

Goals for the Weeks

Affirmations

Wins From Today

The Integrity Driven Leader

Today's Priorities

Gratitude

Meetings & Personal Conferences

Daily Practice

- Exercise/Stretch
- Read/Audio Book
- Pray/Meditate
- Give Recognition
- Relationship Time
- Emotional Intelligence
- Candid Conversations
- Self-Accountability
- Integrity
- Perseverence
- Wise Financial Choices
- Charity/Generosity
- Water Intake
- Eat Right
- Limit TV/Social Media
- Limit Alcohol/Vices
- Healthy Sleep

Goals for the Weeks

Affirmations

Wins From Today

The Integrity Driven Leader

Today's Priorities

Gratitude

Meetings & Personal Conferences

Daily Practice

- Exercise/Stretch
- Read/Audio Book
- Pray/Meditate
- Give Recognition
- Relationship Time
- Emotional Intelligence
- Candid Conversations
- Self-Accountability
- Integrity
- Perseverence
- Wise Financial Choices
- Charity/Generosity
- Water Intake
- Eat Right
- Limit TV/Social Media
- Limit Alcohol/Vices
- Healthy Sleep

Goals for the Weeks

Affirmations

Wins From Today

The Integrity Driven Leader

Today's Priorities

Gratitude

Meetings & Personal Conferences

Daily Practice

- Exercise/Stretch
- Read/Audio Book
- Pray/Meditate
- Give Recognition
- Relationship Time
- Emotional Intelligence
- Candid Conversations
- Self-Accountability
- Integrity
- Perseverence
- Wise Financial Choices
- Charity/Generosity
- Water Intake
- Eat Right
- Limit TV/Social Media
- Limit Alcohol/Vices
- Healthy Sleep

Goals for the Weeks

Affirmations

Wins From Today

The Integrity Driven Leader

Today's Priorities

- ○
- ○
- ○
- ○
- ○
- ○
- ○
- ○
- ○
- ○

Gratitude

Meetings & Personal Conferences

- ○
- ○
- ○
- ○
- ○
- ○

Daily Practice

- ○ Exercise/Stretch
- ○ Read/Audio Book
- ○ Pray/Meditate
- ○ Give Recognition
- ○ Relationship Time
- ○ Emotional Intelligence
- ○ Candid Conversations
- ○ Self-Accountability
- ○ Integrity
- ○ Perseverence
- ○ Wise Financial Choices
- ○ Charity/Generosity
- ○ Water Intake
- ○ Eat Right
- ○ Limit TV/Social Media
- ○ Limit Alcohol/Vices
- ○ Healthy Sleep

Goals for the Weeks

Affirmations

Wins From Today

The Integrity Driven Leader

Today's Priorities

Gratitude

Meetings & Personal Conferences

Daily Practice

- Exercise/Stretch
- Read/Audio Book
- Pray/Meditate
- Give Recognition
- Relationship Time
- Emotional Intelligence
- Candid Conversations
- Self-Accountability
- Integrity
- Perseverence
- Wise Financial Choices
- Charity/Generosity
- Water Intake
- Eat Right
- Limit TV/Social Media
- Limit Alcohol/Vices
- Healthy Sleep

Goals for the Weeks

Affirmations

Wins From Today

The Integrity Driven Leader

Today's Priorities

Gratitude

Meetings & Personal Conferences

Daily Practice

- ○ Exercise/Stretch
- ○ Read/Audio Book
- ○ Pray/Meditate
- ○ Give Recognition
- ○ Relationship Time
- ○ Emotional Intelligence
- ○ Candid Conversations
- ○ Self-Accountability
- ○ Integrity
- ○ Perseverence
- ○ Wise Financial Choices
- ○ Charity/Generosity
- ○ Water Intake
- ○ Eat Right
- ○ Limit TV/Social Media
- ○ Limit Alcohol/Vices
- ○ Healthy Sleep

Goals for the Weeks

Affirmations

Wins From Today

The Integrity Driven Leader

Coaching Action Items

Date Assigned:

Due Date:

Notes:

Inspiration

Areas of Personal Growth

Team Strengths this Period

Team Opportunities this Period

The Integrity Driven Leader

Today's Priorities

Gratitude

Meetings & Personal Conferences

Daily Practice

- Exercise/Stretch
- Read/Audio Book
- Pray/Meditate
- Give Recognition
- Relationship Time
- Emotional Intelligence
- Candid Conversations
- Self-Accountability
- Integrity
- Perseverence
- Wise Financial Choices
- Charity/Generosity
- Water Intake
- Eat Right
- Limit TV/Social Media
- Limit Alcohol/Vices
- Healthy Sleep

Goals for the Weeks

Affirmations

Wins From Today

The Integrity Driven Leader

Today's Priorities

- ○
- ○
- ○
- ○
- ○
- ○
- ○
- ○
- ○
- ○

Gratitude

Meetings & Personal Conferences

- ○
- ○
- ○
- ○
- ○
- ○

Daily Practice

- ○ Exercise/Stretch
- ○ Read/Audio Book
- ○ Pray/Meditate
- ○ Give Recognition
- ○ Relationship Time
- ○ Emotional Intelligence
- ○ Candid Conversations
- ○ Self-Accountability
- ○ Integrity
- ○ Perseverence
- ○ Wise Financial Choices
- ○ Charity/Generosity
- ○ Water Intake
- ○ Eat Right
- ○ Limit TV/Social Media
- ○ Limit Alcohol/Vices
- ○ Healthy Sleep

Goals for the Weeks

Affirmations

Wins From Today

The Integrity Driven Leader

Today's Priorities

- ○
- ○
- ○
- ○
- ○
- ○
- ○
- ○
- ○
- ○

Gratitude

Meetings & Personal Conferences

- ○
- ○
- ○
- ○
- ○
- ○

Daily Practice

- ○ Exercise/Stretch
- ○ Read/Audio Book
- ○ Pray/Meditate
- ○ Give Recognition
- ○ Relationship Time
- ○ Emotional Intelligence
- ○ Candid Conversations
- ○ Self-Accountability
- ○ Integrity
- ○ Perseverence
- ○ Wise Financial Choices
- ○ Charity/Generosity
- ○ Water Intake
- ○ Eat Right
- ○ Limit TV/Social Media
- ○ Limit Alcohol/Vices
- ○ Healthy Sleep

Goals for the Weeks

Affirmations

Wins From Today

The Integrity Driven Leader

Today's Priorities

Gratitude

Meetings & Personal Conferences

Daily Practice

- Exercise/Stretch
- Read/Audio Book
- Pray/Meditate
- Give Recognition
- Relationship Time
- Emotional Intelligence
- Candid Conversations
- Self-Accountability
- Integrity
- Perseverence
- Wise Financial Choices
- Charity/Generosity
- Water Intake
- Eat Right
- Limit TV/Social Media
- Limit Alcohol/Vices
- Healthy Sleep

Goals for the Weeks

Affirmations

Wins From Today

The Integrity Driven Leader

Today's Priorities

Gratitude

Meetings & Personal Conferences

Daily Practice

- Exercise/Stretch
- Read/Audio Book
- Pray/Meditate
- Give Recognition
- Relationship Time
- Emotional Intelligence
- Candid Conversations
- Self-Accountability
- Integrity
- Perseverence
- Wise Financial Choices
- Charity/Generosity
- Water Intake
- Eat Right
- Limit TV/Social Media
- Limit Alcohol/Vices
- Healthy Sleep

Goals for the Weeks

Affirmations

Wins From Today

The Integrity Driven Leader

Today's Priorities

- ○
- ○
- ○
- ○
- ○
- ○
- ○
- ○
- ○
- ○

Gratitude

Meetings & Personal Conferences

- ○
- ○
- ○
- ○
- ○
- ○

Daily Practice

- ○ Exercise/Stretch
- ○ Read/Audio Book
- ○ Pray/Meditate
- ○ Give Recognition
- ○ Relationship Time
- ○ Emotional Intelligence
- ○ Candid Conversations
- ○ Self-Accountability
- ○ Integrity
- ○ Perseverence
- ○ Wise Financial Choices
- ○ Charity/Generosity
- ○ Water Intake
- ○ Eat Right
- ○ Limit TV/Social Media
- ○ Limit Alcohol/Vices
- ○ Healthy Sleep

Goals for the Weeks

Affirmations

Wins From Today

The Integrity Driven Leader

Today's Priorities

- ○
- ○
- ○
- ○
- ○
- ○
- ○
- ○
- ○
- ○

Gratitude

Meetings & Personal Conferences

- ○
- ○
- ○
- ○
- ○
- ○

Daily Practice

- ○ Exercise/Stretch
- ○ Read/Audio Book
- ○ Pray/Meditate
- ○ Give Recognition
- ○ Relationship Time
- ○ Emotional Intelligence
- ○ Candid Conversations
- ○ Self-Accountability
- ○ Integrity
- ○ Perseverence
- ○ Wise Financial Choices
- ○ Charity/Generosity
- ○ Water Intake
- ○ Eat Right
- ○ Limit TV/Social Media
- ○ Limit Alcohol/Vices
- ○ Healthy Sleep

Goals for the Weeks

Affirmations

Wins From Today

The Integrity Driven Leader

Today's Priorities

Gratitude

Meetings & Personal Conferences

Daily Practice

- Exercise/Stretch
- Read/Audio Book
- Pray/Meditate
- Give Recognition
- Relationship Time
- Emotional Intelligence
- Candid Conversations
- Self-Accountability
- Integrity
- Perseverence
- Wise Financial Choices
- Charity/Generosity
- Water Intake
- Eat Right
- Limit TV/Social Media
- Limit Alcohol/Vices
- Healthy Sleep

Goals for the Weeks

Affirmations

Wins From Today

The Integrity Driven Leader

Today's Priorities

- ○
- ○
- ○
- ○
- ○
- ○
- ○
- ○
- ○
- ○

Gratitude

Meetings & Personal Conferences

- ○
- ○
- ○
- ○
- ○
- ○

Daily Practice

- ○ Exercise/Stretch
- ○ Read/Audio Book
- ○ Pray/Meditate
- ○ Give Recognition
- ○ Relationship Time
- ○ Emotional Intelligence
- ○ Candid Conversations
- ○ Self-Accountability
- ○ Integrity
- ○ Perseverence
- ○ Wise Financial Choices
- ○ Charity/Generosity
- ○ Water Intake
- ○ Eat Right
- ○ Limit TV/Social Media
- ○ Limit Alcohol/Vices
- ○ Healthy Sleep

Goals for the Weeks

Affirmations

Wins From Today

The Integrity Driven Leader

Today's Priorities

Gratitude

Meetings & Personal Conferences

Daily Practice

- ○ Exercise/Stretch
- ○ Read/Audio Book
- ○ Pray/Meditate
- ○ Give Recognition
- ○ Relationship Time
- ○ Emotional Intelligence
- ○ Candid Conversations
- ○ Self-Accountability
- ○ Integrity
- ○ Perseverence
- ○ Wise Financial Choices
- ○ Charity/Generosity
- ○ Water Intake
- ○ Eat Right
- ○ Limit TV/Social Media
- ○ Limit Alcohol/Vices
- ○ Healthy Sleep

Goals for the Weeks

Affirmations

Wins From Today

The Integrity Driven Leader

Coaching Action Items

Date Assigned:

Due Date:

Notes:

- ○
- ○
- ○
- ○
- ○

Inspiration

Areas of Personal Growth

- ○
- ○
- ○
- ○
- ○
- ○
- ○
- ○

Team Strengths this Period

- ○
- ○
- ○
- ○

Team Opportunities this Period

- ○
- ○
- ○
- ○

The Integrity Driven Leader

Today's Priorities

Gratitude

Meetings & Personal Conferences

Daily Practice

- Exercise/Stretch
- Read/Audio Book
- Pray/Meditate
- Give Recognition
- Relationship Time
- Emotional Intelligence
- Candid Conversations
- Self-Accountability
- Integrity
- Perseverence
- Wise Financial Choices
- Charity/Generosity
- Water Intake
- Eat Right
- Limit TV/Social Media
- Limit Alcohol/Vices
- Healthy Sleep

Goals for the Weeks

Affirmations

Wins From Today

The Integrity Driven Leader

Today's Priorities

- ○
- ○
- ○
- ○
- ○
- ○
- ○
- ○
- ○
- ○

Gratitude

Meetings & Personal Conferences

- ○
- ○
- ○
- ○
- ○
- ○

Daily Practice

- ○ Exercise/Stretch
- ○ Read/Audio Book
- ○ Pray/Meditate
- ○ Give Recognition
- ○ Relationship Time
- ○ Emotional Intelligence
- ○ Candid Conversations
- ○ Self-Accountability
- ○ Integrity
- ○ Perseverence
- ○ Wise Financial Choices
- ○ Charity/Generosity
- ○ Water Intake
- ○ Eat Right
- ○ Limit TV/Social Media
- ○ Limit Alcohol/Vices
- ○ Healthy Sleep

Goals for the Weeks

Affirmations

Wins From Today

The Integrity Driven Leader

Today's Priorities

Gratitude

Meetings & Personal Conferences

Daily Practice

- Exercise/Stretch
- Read/Audio Book
- Pray/Meditate
- Give Recognition
- Relationship Time
- Emotional Intelligence
- Candid Conversations
- Self-Accountability
- Integrity
- Perseverence
- Wise Financial Choices
- Charity/Generosity
- Water Intake
- Eat Right
- Limit TV/Social Media
- Limit Alcohol/Vices
- Healthy Sleep

Goals for the Weeks

Affirmations

Wins From Today

The Integrity Driven Leader

Today's Priorities

Gratitude

Meetings & Personal Conferences

Daily Practice

- Exercise/Stretch
- Read/Audio Book
- Pray/Meditate
- Give Recognition
- Relationship Time
- Emotional Intelligence
- Candid Conversations
- Self-Accountability
- Integrity
- Perseverence
- Wise Financial Choices
- Charity/Generosity
- Water Intake
- Eat Right
- Limit TV/Social Media
- Limit Alcohol/Vices
- Healthy Sleep

Goals for the Weeks

Affirmations

Wins From Today

The Integrity Driven Leader

Today's Priorities

Gratitude

Meetings & Personal Conferences

Daily Practice

- Exercise/Stretch
- Read/Audio Book
- Pray/Meditate
- Give Recognition
- Relationship Time
- Emotional Intelligence
- Candid Conversations
- Self-Accountability
- Integrity
- Perseverence
- Wise Financial Choices
- Charity/Generosity
- Water Intake
- Eat Right
- Limit TV/Social Media
- Limit Alcohol/Vices
- Healthy Sleep

Goals for the Weeks

Affirmations

Wins From Today

The Integrity Driven Leader

Today's Priorities

- ○
- ○
- ○
- ○
- ○
- ○
- ○
- ○
- ○
- ○

Gratitude

Meetings & Personal Conferences

- ○
- ○
- ○
- ○
- ○
- ○

Daily Practice

- ○ Exercise/Stretch
- ○ Read/Audio Book
- ○ Pray/Meditate
- ○ Give Recognition
- ○ Relationship Time
- ○ Emotional Intelligence
- ○ Candid Conversations
- ○ Self-Accountability
- ○ Integrity
- ○ Perseverence
- ○ Wise Financial Choices
- ○ Charity/Generosity
- ○ Water Intake
- ○ Eat Right
- ○ Limit TV/Social Media
- ○ Limit Alcohol/Vices
- ○ Healthy Sleep

Goals for the Weeks

Affirmations

Wins From Today

The Integrity Driven Leader

Today's Priorities

- ○
- ○
- ○
- ○
- ○
- ○
- ○
- ○
- ○
- ○

Gratitude

Meetings & Personal Conferences

- ○
- ○
- ○
- ○
- ○
- ○

Daily Practice

- ○ Exercise/Stretch
- ○ Read/Audio Book
- ○ Pray/Meditate
- ○ Give Recognition
- ○ Relationship Time
- ○ Emotional Intelligence
- ○ Candid Conversations
- ○ Self-Accountability
- ○ Integrity
- ○ Perseverence
- ○ Wise Financial Choices
- ○ Charity/Generosity
- ○ Water Intake
- ○ Eat Right
- ○ Limit TV/Social Media
- ○ Limit Alcohol/Vices
- ○ Healthy Sleep

Goals for the Weeks

Affirmations

Wins From Today

The Integrity Driven Leader

Today's Priorities

Gratitude

Meetings & Personal Conferences

Daily Practice

- Exercise/Stretch
- Read/Audio Book
- Pray/Meditate
- Give Recognition
- Relationship Time
- Emotional Intelligence
- Candid Conversations
- Self-Accountability
- Integrity
- Perseverence
- Wise Financial Choices
- Charity/Generosity
- Water Intakc
- Eat Right
- Limit TV/Social Media
- Limit Alcohol/Vices
- Healthy Sleep

Goals for the Weeks

Affirmations

Wins From Today

The Integrity Driven Leader

Today's Priorities

Gratitude

Meetings & Personal Conferences

Daily Practice

- Exercise/Stretch
- Read/Audio Book
- Pray/Meditate
- Give Recognition
- Relationship Time
- Emotional Intelligence
- Candid Conversations
- Self-Accountability
- Integrity
- Perseverence
- Wise Financial Choices
- Charity/Generosity
- Water Intake
- Eat Right
- Limit TV/Social Media
- Limit Alcohol/Vices
- Healthy Sleep

Goals for the Weeks

Affirmations

Wins From Today

The Integrity Driven Leader

Today's Priorities

Gratitude

Meetings & Personal Conferences

Daily Practice

- Exercise/Stretch
- Read/Audio Book
- Pray/Meditate
- Give Recognition
- Relationship Time
- Emotional Intelligence
- Candid Conversations
- Self-Accountability
- Integrity
- Perseverence
- Wise Financial Choices
- Charity/Generosity
- Water Intake
- Eat Right
- Limit TV/Social Media
- Limit Alcohol/Vices
- Healthy Sleep

Goals for the Weeks

Affirmations

Wins From Today

The Integrity Driven Leader

Coaching Action Items

Date Assigned:

Due Date:

Notes:

Inspiration

Areas of Personal Growth

Team Strengths this Period

Team Opportunities this Period

The Integrity Driven Leader

Today's Priorities

Gratitude

Meetings & Personal Conferences

Daily Practice

- Exercise/Stretch
- Read/Audio Book
- Pray/Meditate
- Give Recognition
- Relationship Time
- Emotional Intelligence
- Candid Conversations
- Self-Accountability
- Integrity
- Perseverence
- Wise Financial Choices
- Charity/Generosity
- Water Intake
- Eat Right
- Limit TV/Social Media
- Limit Alcohol/Vices
- Healthy Sleep

Goals for the Weeks

Affirmations

Wins From Today

The Integrity Driven Leader

Today's Priorities

Gratitude

Meetings & Personal Conferences

Daily Practice

- Exercise/Stretch
- Read/Audio Book
- Pray/Meditate
- Give Recognition
- Relationship Time
- Emotional Intelligence
- Candid Conversations
- Self-Accountability
- Integrity
- Perseverence
- Wise Financial Choices
- Charity/Generosity
- Water Intake
- Eat Right
- Limit TV/Social Media
- Limit Alcohol/Vices
- Healthy Sleep

Goals for the Weeks

Affirmations

Wins From Today

The Integrity Driven Leader

Today's Priorities

Gratitude

Meetings & Personal Conferences

Daily Practice

- Exercise/Stretch
- Read/Audio Book
- Pray/Meditate
- Give Recognition
- Relationship Time
- Emotional Intelligence
- Candid Conversations
- Self-Accountability
- Integrity
- Perseverence
- Wise Financial Choices
- Charity/Generosity
- Water Intake
- Eat Right
- Limit TV/Social Media
- Limit Alcohol/Vices
- Healthy Sleep

Goals for the Weeks

Affirmations

Wins From Today

The Integrity Driven Leader

Today's Priorities

Gratitude

Meetings & Personal Conferences

Daily Practice

- Exercise/Stretch
- Read/Audio Book
- Pray/Meditate
- Give Recognition
- Relationship Time
- Emotional Intelligence
- Candid Conversations
- Self-Accountability
- Integrity
- Perseverence
- Wise Financial Choices
- Charity/Generosity
- Water Intake
- Eat Right
- Limit TV/Social Media
- Limit Alcohol/Vices
- Healthy Sleep

Goals for the Weeks

Affirmations

Wins From Today

The Integrity Driven Leader

Today's Priorities

- [ ]
- [ ]
- [ ]
- [ ]
- [ ]
- [ ]
- [ ]
- [ ]
- [ ]
- [ ]

Gratitude

Meetings & Personal Conferences

- [ ]
- [ ]
- [ ]
- [ ]
- [ ]
- [ ]

Daily Practice

- [ ] Exercise/Stretch
- [ ] Read/Audio Book
- [ ] Pray/Meditate
- [ ] Give Recognition
- [ ] Relationship Time
- [ ] Emotional Intelligence
- [ ] Candid Conversations
- [ ] Self-Accountability
- [ ] Integrity
- [ ] Perseverence
- [ ] Wise Financial Choices
- [ ] Charity/Generosity
- [ ] Water Intake
- [ ] Eat Right
- [ ] Limit TV/Social Media
- [ ] Limit Alcohol/Vices
- [ ] Healthy Sleep

Goals for the Weeks

Affirmations

Wins From Today

The Integrity Driven Leader

Today's Priorities

Gratitude

Meetings & Personal Conferences

Daily Practice

- Exercise/Stretch
- Read/Audio Book
- Pray/Meditate
- Give Recognition
- Relationship Time
- Emotional Intelligence
- Candid Conversations
- Self-Accountability
- Integrity
- Perseverence
- Wise Financial Choices
- Charity/Generosity
- Water Intake
- Eat Right
- Limit TV/Social Media
- Limit Alcohol/Vices
- Healthy Sleep

Goals for the Weeks

Affirmations

Wins From Today

The Integrity Driven Leader

Today's Priorities

Gratitude

Meetings & Personal Conferences

Daily Practice

- Exercise/Stretch
- Read/Audio Book
- Pray/Meditate
- Give Recognition
- Relationship Time
- Emotional Intelligence
- Candid Conversations
- Self-Accountability
- Integrity
- Perseverence
- Wise Financial Choices
- Charity/Generosity
- Water Intake
- Eat Right
- Limit TV/Social Media
- Limit Alcohol/Vices
- Healthy Sleep

Goals for the Weeks

Affirmations

Wins From Today

The Integrity Driven Leader

Today's Priorities

Gratitude

Meetings & Personal Conferences

Daily Practice

- Exercise/Stretch
- Read/Audio Book
- Pray/Meditate
- Give Recognition
- Relationship Time
- Emotional Intelligence
- Candid Conversations
- Self-Accountability
- Integrity
- Perseverence
- Wise Financial Choices
- Charity/Generosity
- Water Intake
- Eat Right
- Limit TV/Social Media
- Limit Alcohol/Vices
- Healthy Sleep

Goals for the Weeks

Affirmations

Wins From Today

The Integrity Driven Leader

Today's Priorities

Gratitude

Meetings & Personal Conferences

Daily Practice

- Exercise/Stretch
- Read/Audio Book
- Pray/Meditate
- Give Recognition
- Relationship Time
- Emotional Intelligence
- Candid Conversations
- Self-Accountability
- Integrity
- Perseverence
- Wise Financial Choices
- Charity/Generosity
- Water Intake
- Eat Right
- Limit TV/Social Media
- Limit Alcohol/Vices
- Healthy Sleep

Goals for the Weeks

Affirmations

Wins From Today

The Integrity Driven Leader

Today's Priorities

Gratitude

Meetings & Personal Conferences

Daily Practice

- Exercise/Stretch
- Read/Audio Book
- Pray/Meditate
- Give Recognition
- Relationship Time
- Emotional Intelligence
- Candid Conversations
- Self-Accountability
- Integrity
- Perseverence
- Wise Financial Choices
- Charity/Generosity
- Water Intake
- Eat Right
- Limit TV/Social Media
- Limit Alcohol/Vices
- Healthy Sleep

Goals for the Weeks

Affirmations

Wins From Today

The Integrity Driven Leader

Time to Order Your Next Journal

We hope you are enjoying your journal and seeing the payoff of daily planning, bi-weekly strategy, and quarterly vision refinement.

Here's to your next season of growth in business and in life!

Order your next copy now on Amazon!

"Creating a culture of integrity and accountability not only improves effectiveness, it also generates a respectful, enjoyable and life-giving setting in which to work."
Tom Hanson

"Six essential qualities that are the key to success: Sincerity, personal integrity, humility, courtesy, wisdom, charity."
Dr. William Menninger

"The qualities of a great man are "vision, integrity, courage, understanding, the power of articulation, and profundity of character."
Dwight Eisenhower

"Integrity is the seed for achievement. It is the principle that never fails."
Earl Nightingale

Order Your Next Journal **Today!**

The Integrity Driven Leader

Coaching Action Items

Date Assigned:

Due Date:

Notes:

Inspiration

Areas of Personal Growth

Team Strengths this Period

Team Opportunities this Period

The Integrity Driven Leader

Today's Priorities

Gratitude

Meetings & Personal Conferences

Daily Practice

- Exercise/Stretch
- Read/Audio Book
- Pray/Meditate
- Give Recognition
- Relationship Time
- Emotional Intelligence
- Candid Conversations
- Self-Accountability
- Integrity
- Perseverence
- Wise Financial Choices
- Charity/Generosity
- Water Intake
- Eat Right
- Limit TV/Social Media
- Limit Alcohol/Vices
- Healthy Sleep

Goals for the Weeks

Affirmations

Wins From Today

The Integrity Driven Leader

Today's Priorities

- ○
- ○
- ○
- ○
- ○
- ○
- ○
- ○
- ○
- ○

Gratitude

Meetings & Personal Conferences

- ○
- ○
- ○
- ○
- ○
- ○

Daily Practice

- ○ Exercise/Stretch
- ○ Read/Audio Book
- ○ Pray/Meditate
- ○ Give Recognition
- ○ Relationship Time
- ○ Emotional Intelligence
- ○ Candid Conversations
- ○ Self-Accountability
- ○ Integrity
- ○ Perseverence
- ○ Wise Financial Choices
- ○ Charity/Generosity
- ○ Water Intake
- ○ Eat Right
- ○ Limit TV/Social Media
- ○ Limit Alcohol/Vices
- ○ Healthy Sleep

Goals for the Weeks

Affirmations

Wins From Today

The Integrity Driven Leader

Today's Priorities

Gratitude

Meetings & Personal Conferences

Daily Practice

- Exercise/Stretch
- Read/Audio Book
- Pray/Meditate
- Give Recognition
- Relationship Time
- Emotional Intelligence
- Candid Conversations
- Self-Accountability
- Integrity
- Perseverence
- Wise Financial Choices
- Charity/Generosity
- Water Intake
- Eat Right
- Limit TV/Social Media
- Limit Alcohol/Vices
- Healthy Sleep

Goals for the Weeks

Affirmations

Wins From Today

The Integrity Driven Leader

Today's Priorities

Gratitude

Meetings & Personal Conferences

Daily Practice

- Exercise/Stretch
- Read/Audio Book
- Pray/Meditate
- Give Recognition
- Relationship Time
- Emotional Intelligence
- Candid Conversations
- Self-Accountability
- Integrity
- Perseverence
- Wise Financial Choices
- Charity/Generosity
- Water Intake
- Eat Right
- Limit TV/Social Media
- Limit Alcohol/Vices
- Healthy Sleep

Goals for the Weeks

Affirmations

Wins From Today

The Integrity Driven Leader

Today's Priorities

- ○
- ○
- ○
- ○
- ○
- ○
- ○
- ○
- ○
- ○

Gratitude

Meetings & Personal Conferences

- ○
- ○
- ○
- ○
- ○
- ○

Daily Practice

- ○ Exercise/Stretch
- ○ Read/Audio Book
- ○ Pray/Meditate
- ○ Give Recognition
- ○ Relationship Time
- ○ Emotional Intelligence
- ○ Candid Conversations
- ○ Self-Accountability
- ○ Integrity
- ○ Perseverence
- ○ Wise Financial Choices
- ○ Charity/Generosity
- ○ Water Intake
- ○ Eat Right
- ○ Limit TV/Social Media
- ○ Limit Alcohol/Vices
- ○ Healthy Sleep

Goals for the Weeks

Affirmations

Wins From Today

The Integrity Driven Leader

Today's Priorities

- ○
- ○
- ○
- ○
- ○
- ○
- ○
- ○
- ○
- ○

Gratitude

Meetings & Personal Conferences

- ○
- ○
- ○
- ○
- ○
- ○

Daily Practice

- ○ Exercise/Stretch
- ○ Read/Audio Book
- ○ Pray/Meditate
- ○ Give Recognition
- ○ Relationship Time
- ○ Emotional Intelligence
- ○ Candid Conversations
- ○ Self-Accountability
- ○ Integrity
- ○ Perseverence
- ○ Wise Financial Choices
- ○ Charity/Generosity
- ○ Water Intake
- ○ Eat Right
- ○ Limit TV/Social Media
- ○ Limit Alcohol/Vices
- ○ Healthy Sleep

Goals for the Weeks

Affirmations

Wins From Today

The Integrity Driven Leader

Today's Priorities

Gratitude

Meetings & Personal Conferences

Daily Practice

- Exercise/Stretch
- Read/Audio Book
- Pray/Meditate
- Give Recognition
- Relationship Time
- Emotional Intelligence
- Candid Conversations
- Self-Accountability
- Integrity
- Perseverence
- Wise Financial Choices
- Charity/Generosity
- Water Intake
- Eat Right
- Limit TV/Social Media
- Limit Alcohol/Vices
- Healthy Sleep

Goals for the Weeks

Affirmations

Wins From Today

The Integrity Driven Leader

Today's Priorities

Gratitude

Meetings & Personal Conferences

Daily Practice

- Exercise/Stretch
- Read/Audio Book
- Pray/Meditate
- Give Recognition
- Relationship Time
- Emotional Intelligence
- Candid Conversations
- Self-Accountability
- Integrity
- Perseverence
- Wise Financial Choices
- Charity/Generosity
- Water Intake
- Eat Right
- Limit TV/Social Media
- Limit Alcohol/Vices
- Healthy Sleep

Goals for the Weeks

Affirmations

Wins From Today

The Integrity Driven Leader

Today's Priorities

Gratitude

Meetings & Personal Conferences

Daily Practice

- Exercise/Stretch
- Read/Audio Book
- Pray/Meditate
- Give Recognition
- Relationship Time
- Emotional Intelligence
- Candid Conversations
- Self-Accountability
- Integrity
- Perseverence
- Wise Financial Choices
- Charity/Generosity
- Water Intake
- Eat Right
- Limit TV/Social Media
- Limit Alcohol/Vices
- Healthy Sleep

Goals for the Weeks

Affirmations

Wins From Today

The Integrity Driven Leader

Today's Priorities

- ○
- ○
- ○
- ○
- ○
- ○
- ○
- ○
- ○
- ○

Gratitude

Meetings & Personal Conferences

- ○
- ○
- ○
- ○
- ○
- ○

Daily Practice

- ○ Exercise/Stretch
- ○ Read/Audio Book
- ○ Pray/Meditate
- ○ Give Recognition
- ○ Relationship Time
- ○ Emotional Intelligence
- ○ Candid Conversations
- ○ Self-Accountability
- ○ Integrity
- ○ Perseverence
- ○ Wise Financial Choices
- ○ Charity/Generosity
- ○ Water Intake
- ○ Eat Right
- ○ Limit TV/Social Media
- ○ Limit Alcohol/Vices
- ○ Healthy Sleep

Goals for the Weeks

Affirmations

Wins From Today